HOW TO BECOME RICH.
1 Specialize in something obscure, then find a patron.
2 Slather your body in coconut oil, then pray to your god for money to rain down upon you.
(This has worked once before.)
3 Only befriend rich people; learn their secrets, then write a book about them.
BONUS POINTS:
Become a traveling motivational speaker. This can bring in the big bucks.
4 Legally wed a million-dollar bill. Make lots of babies.

STICK THAT STAMP HERE

30 Ways to Annoy Your Friends by Mail

from 120 Ways to Annoy Your Mother (and Influence People),
published by Thames & Hudson

Thames & Hudson

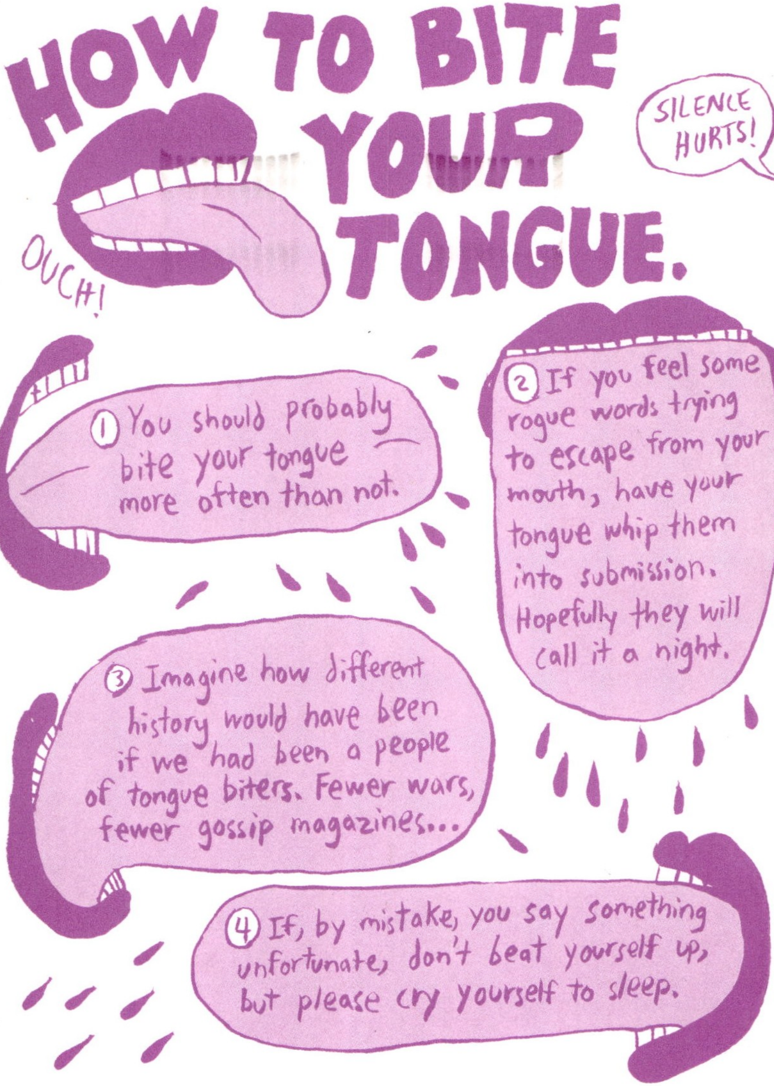
HOW TO BITE YOUR TONGUE.
SILENCE HURTS!
OUCH!
① You should probably bite your tongue more often than not.
② If you feel some rogue words trying to escape from your mouth, have your tongue whip them into submission. Hopefully they will call it a night.
③ Imagine how different history would have been if we had been a people of tongue biters. Fewer wars, fewer gossip magazines...
④ If, by mistake, you say something unfortunate, don't beat yourself up, but please cry yourself to sleep.

STICK
THAT
STAMP
HERE

30 Ways to Annoy Your Friends by Mail
Illustration © 2014 Ana Benaroya
from *120 Ways to Annoy Your Mother (and Influence People)*,
published by Thames & Hudson

Thames & Hudson

HOW TO APPRECIATE WHAT YOU HAVE.

1 Constantly stare at your few possessions. They are beautiful and lovely.

2 Name each one of the objects you own. Speak to them as though they are people.

3 Only befriend people who own fewer things than you.

4 Lick everything. Leave your scent on each and every item. Mark your TERRITORY!

STICK
THAT
STAMP
HERE

30 Ways to Annoy Your Friends by Mail
Illustration © 2014 Ana Benaroya
from 120 Ways to Annoy Your Mother (and Influence People),
published by Thames & Hudson

Thames & Hudson

HOW TO CURL YOUR EYE LASHES.

1. Condition them first with a potion of baby's tears and warm butter.
2. Massage them gently upwards for six to eight hours. Do not break.
3. Deep within your soul, imagine gravity has reversed and what was once down is now up.
4. Come up with a name for each eyelash, then mourn its death when it falls off.

STICK THAT STAMP HERE

30 Ways to Annoy Your Friends by Mail
Illustration © 2014 Ana Benaroya
from 120 Ways to Annoy Your Mother (and Influence People),
published by Thames & Hudson

Thames & Hudson

HOW ALWAYS TO HAVE THE ANSWER.

1. Remember, answers do not have to be right.

2. Follow this cardinal rule: Those who are the loudest are the rightest.

3. Answers are never found in books, they are always found in your head. You were born with them.

4. Practice your "all-knowing" face in the mirror.

STICK THAT STAMP HERE

30 Ways to Annoy Your Friends by Mail
Illustration © 2014 Ana Benaroya
from *120 Ways to Annoy Your Mother (and Influence People)*,
published by Thames & Hudson

Thames & Hudson

HOW TO WRITE AN AUTOBIOGRAPHY.

① Keep the book's focus 100% on you. Beautiful, wonderful, intelligent, you!

② Find the overarching heroic theme of your life. If there isn't one, create it.

③ Live each day like a new chapter. If necessary, narrate your day in the third person.

④ Take creative liberties. No one will know you weren't actually the center of the universe.

STICK
THAT
STAMP
HERE

30 Ways to Annoy Your Friends by Mail
from 120 Ways to Annoy Your Mother (and Influence People),
published by Thames & Hudson

Thames & Hudson

HOW TO APPRECIATE JAZZ MUSIC.
1 Make that face. You know which face I'm talking about.
2 Put a little bounce in your every step.
3 Speak in a syncopated rhythm. No, PEOPLE will NOT think YOU'RE strange.
4 Doobie doobie doo. Zap bap a doo beep! BOP!

STICK THAT STAMP HERE

30 Ways to Annoy Your Friends by Mail
Illustration © 2014 Ana Benaroya
from 120 Ways to Annoy Your Mother (and Influence People),
published by Thames & Hudson
Thames & Hudson

HOW TO PRETEND YOU ARE REALLY INTERESTED IN SOMETHING SOMEONE IS TALKING ABOUT.

1. Constantly nod and maintain eye contact with their right eyeball.

2. Have a set of generic phrases that you can call upon if you need to respond.

   Ex: "Mmmh mmm."

3. Sync your circadian rhythm with their circadian rhythm.

4. Take notes. Dispose of them before bed.

STICK THAT STAMP HERE

30 Ways to Annoy Your Friends by Mail
Illustration © 2014 Ana Benaroya
from 120 Ways to Annoy Your Mother (and Influence People),
published by Thames & Hudson

Thames & Hudson

HOW TO GROW A UNIBROW.

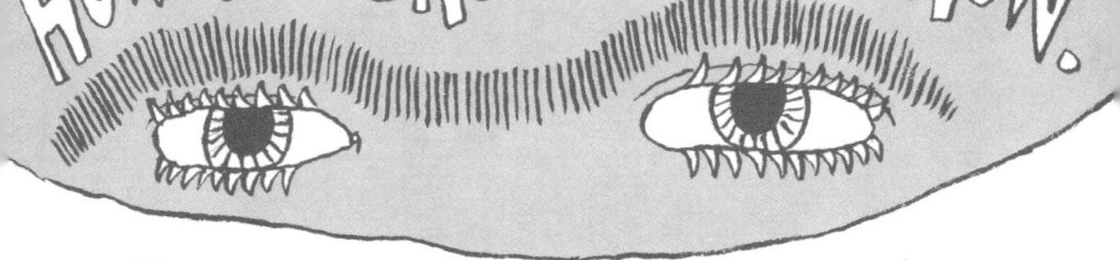

1. Stroke and caress your each and every eyebrow hair follicle.

2. Encourage your eyebrow hairs to start having babies.

3. Write a love letter to the eyebrow god. Beg for an abundant and fruitful unibrow, Amen.

4. Allow your unibrow to pick what to watch on TV every now and then.

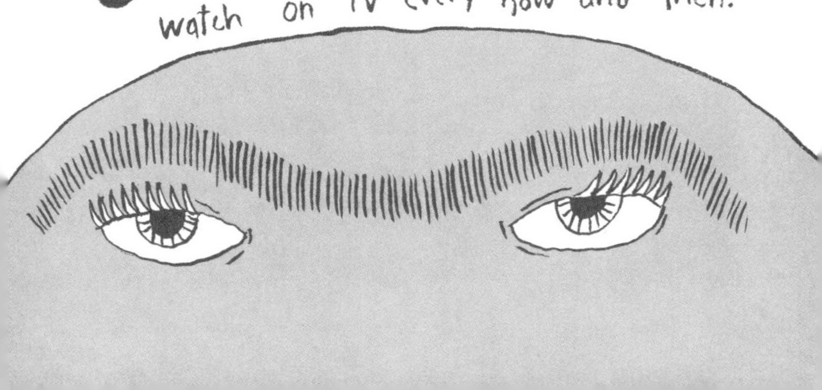

STICK
THAT
STAMP
HERE

30 Ways to Annoy Your Friends by Mail
Illustration © 2014 Ana Benaroya
from 120 Ways to Annoy Your Mother (and Influence People),
published by Thames & Hudson

Thames & Hudson

HOW TO BE A LITTLE BAD (ONLY A LITTLE).

1. Allow yourself to drink diet soda.

2. On a whim, recklessly decide to buy yourself a bagel with cream cheese on your way to work.

3. Stay up late reading your emails.

4. Don't cut your fingernails for two weeks.

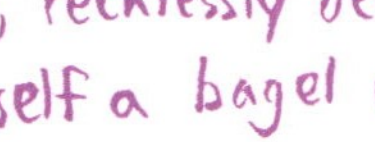

STICK
THAT
STAMP
HERE

30 Ways to Annoy Your Friends by Mail
Illustration © 2014 Ana Benaroya
from 120 Ways to Annoy Your Mother (and Influence People),
Published by Thames & Hudson

Thames & Hudson

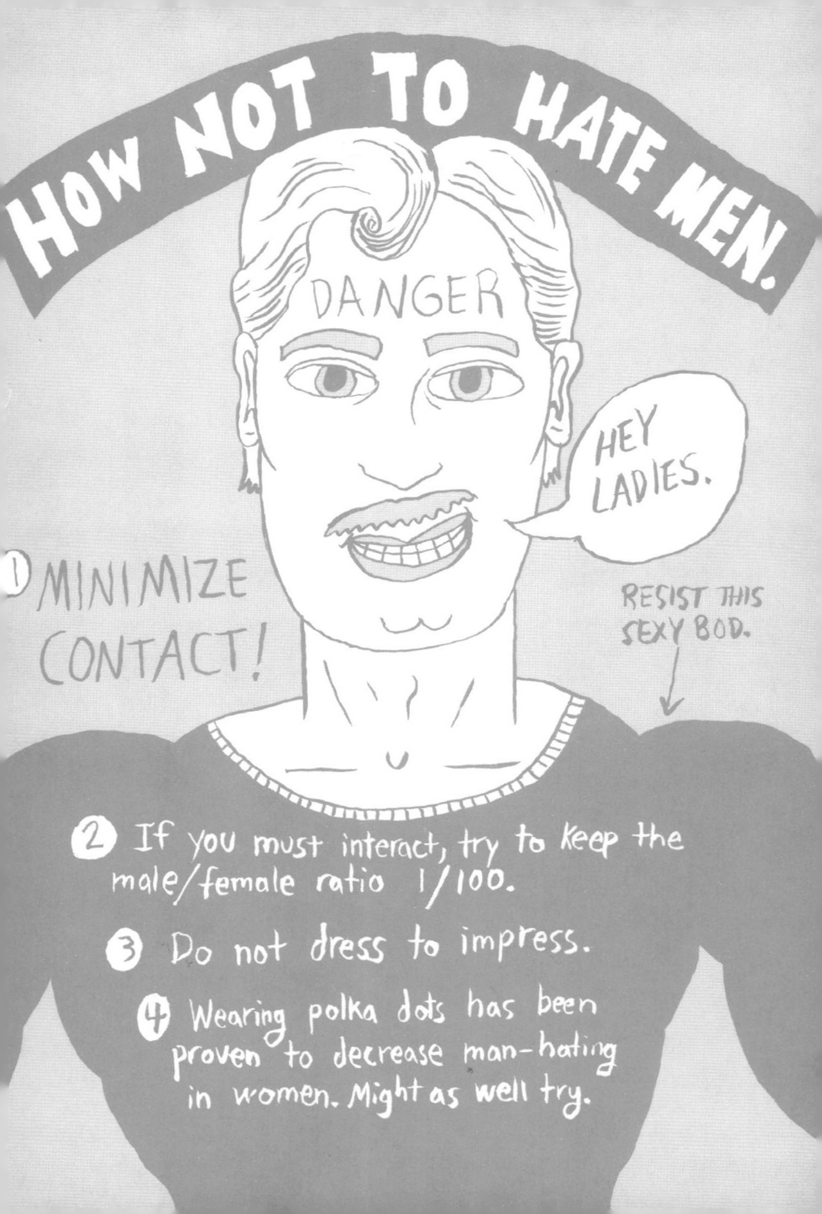

HOW NOT TO HATE MEN.
DANGER
HEY LADIES.
1) MINIMIZE CONTACT!
RESIST THIS SEXY BOD.
2 If you must interact, try to keep the male/female ratio 1/100.
3 Do not dress to impress.
4 Wearing polka dots has been proven to decrease man-hating in women. Might as well try.

STICK
THAT
STAMP
HERE

30 Ways to Annoy Your Friends by Mail
Illustration © 2014 Ana Benaroya
from 120 Ways to Annoy Your Mother (and Influence People),
published by Thames & Hudson

Thames & Hudson

HOW TO PRETEND YOU REALLY LIKE SOMEONE.

1 Shower them with gifts until they become buried underneath a pile of them.

2 Compliment them on superficial things. ("You've got good breath!" or "Your hair looks clean!")

3 Sit next to them during class, but minimize conversation. ("Sorry, I need silence to focus.")

4 Smile as you pass them in the hallway. They probably won't notice the dead look behind your eyes.

STICK THAT STAMP HERE

30 Ways to Annoy Your Friends by Mail
Illustration © 2014 Ana Benaroya
from *120 Ways to Annoy Your Mother (and Influence People)*,
published by Thames & Hudson

Thames & Hudson

HOW TO FIGURE OUT THE MEANING OF LIFE
1 Figuring out the meaning of life might actually be the meaning of life.
2 Try not to get discouraged. Be sure to eat lots of snacks.
3 The meaning of life can hide in all sorts of places. It's often found in cereal boxes.
4 Once you figure it out, be sure to impose your beliefs on everyone you come across.
A megaphone really helps!

STICK
THAT
STAMP
HERE

30 Ways to Annoy Your Friends by Mail
Illustration © 2014 Ana Benaroya
from 120 Ways to Annoy Your Mother (and Influence People),
published by Thames & Hudson

Thames & Hudson

HOW TO TRANSFORM INTO A FISH.

1. Transition slowly by first becoming a mermaid.

2. Try to hang out with some of the local fish in your neighborhood. See if you fit in.

3. Rub your hands together really quickly and see if you grow scales. ← (Known method.)

4. Most importantly, you must read the latest handbook on fish life: "Being a Fish in the Modern Ocean, 12th edition."

STICK
THAT
STAMP
HERE

30 Ways to Annoy Your Friends by Mail
Illustration © 2014 Ana Benaroya
from *120 Ways to Annoy Your Mother (and Influence People)*,
published by Thames & Hudson
Thames & Hudson

HOW TO BE A HERMIT.

1 Becoming a hermit can happen overnight. Sleep the wrong way and next morning you will wake up a hermit.

2 If you find yourself growing sick of humanity, or the lack thereof, being a hermit might be for you.

3 There is one cardinal rule of hermiting that you must follow always: Never talk to people.

4 Home is where the hermit is, so be sure to keep it clean and smelling fresh. No one likes a smelly hermit.

If they know you exist!

STICK THAT STAMP HERE

30 Ways to Annoy Your Friends by Mail

from *120 Ways to Annoy Your Mother (and Influence People)*,
published by Thames & Hudson

Thames & Hudson

HOW TO LIVE A BOHEMIAN LIFESTYLE.

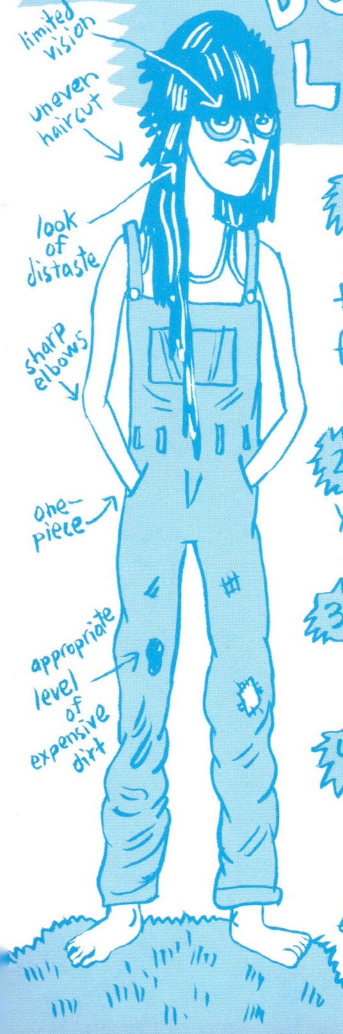

1. Make sure all your friends are also bohemian. If not, it's time to start cutting ties. Even free spirits can be cruel and judgmental.

2. Your possessions should advance your bohemian ways. Being stylish is a must.

3. Formulate strong opinions on modern art and culture. No research necessary.

4. Live in the most bohemian neighborhood possible.

If you can't afford this you are not bohemian.

STICK
THAT
STAMP
HERE

30 Ways to Annoy Your Friends by Mail

from 120 Ways to Annoy Your Mother (and Influence People),
published by Thames & Hudson

Thames & Hudson

OMG!!!

sigh

I LOVE YOU!!!

MARRY ME!!!

EEEEEEE EEEEEEEE EEEEEEEE EEEEEEE!!

HOW TO START YOUR OWN FAN CLUB.

1. Identify your celebrity persona and embody it. Mind, body, and soul.

2. Be elusive and always leave people desiring more.

3. Be the person that everyone loathes and loves. They can't stand you, but want to know everything about you.

4. Sell merchandise with your face on it.

BONUS TIP: Endorse products even if you aren't asked to.

STICK THAT STAMP HERE

30 Ways to Annoy Your Friends by Mail
Illustration © 2014 Ana Benaroya
from *120 Ways to Annoy Your Mother (and Influence People)*,
published by Thames & Hudson
Thames & Hudson

HOW TO TELEPORT.

1. Teleporting is much easier when you're in a good mood.

2. Your particles will need a little motivation to disassemble and reassemble. Buy them a few donuts.

3. Teleportation pads are great, but your shower will work just fine. (Remember, twist the shower head to the right three times.)

4. Do not believe those teleportation diets you see on TV. No, you cannot leave fat particles behind!!

STICK
THAT
STAMP
HERE

30 Ways to Annoy Your Friends by Mail
Illustration © 2014 Ana Benaroya
from 120 Ways to Annoy Your Mother (and Influence People),
published by Thames & Hudson

Thames & Hudson

HOW TO BE REBELLIOUS WITHIN THE CONFINES OF SOCIETY.
1 Join whatever counter-culture movement may be going on ... in your mind.
2 Drink tap water and wear ill-fitting clothing. It's the small things.
3 Push people's metaphysical boundaries.
4 Randomly get really self-righteous, then quickly concede.
FIGHT THE POWER (only a little)
I HATE LOVE THE MAN!

STICK
THAT
STAMP
HERE

30 Ways to Annoy Your Friends by Mail

from 120 Ways to Annoy Your Mother (and Influence People),
published by Thames & Hudson

Thames & Hudson

HOW TO TRANSITION INTO ADULTHOOD.

1. This transition is actually optional.

2. Start lying about your age from the age of ten. If people question you, tell them you were born with a condition.

3. To practice, wear business casual every Friday, starting in middle school.

4. Reminisce about the good old days, even if the good old days involved wearing diapers.

STICK
THAT
STAMP
HERE

30 Ways to Annoy Your Friends by Mail
Illustration © 2014 Ana Benaroya
from 120 Ways to Annoy Your Mother (and Influence People),
published by Thames & Hudson

Thames & Hudson

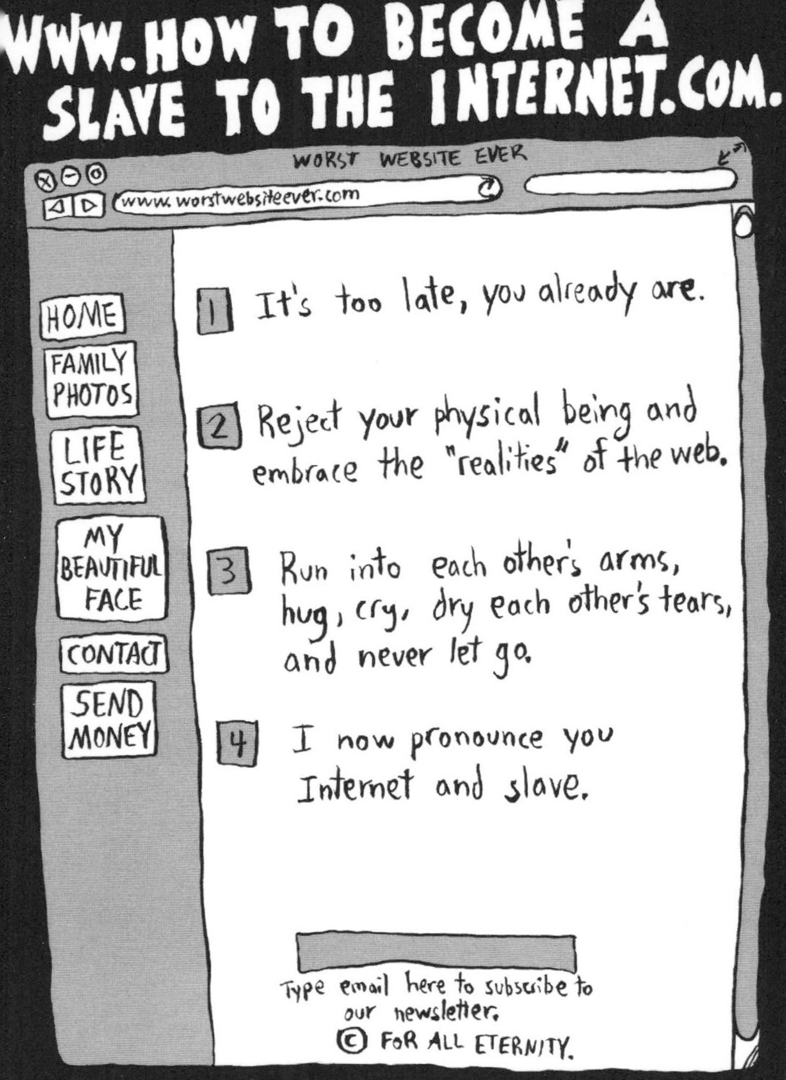
WWW.HOW TO BECOME A SLAVE TO THE INTERNET.COM.
WORST WEBSITE EVER
www.worstwebsiteever.com
HOME
FAMILY PHOTOS
LIFE STORY
MY BEAUTIFUL FACE
CONTACT
SEND MONEY
1 It's too late, you already are.
2 Reject your physical being and embrace the "realities" of the web.
3 Run into each other's arms, hug, cry, dry each other's tears, and never let go.
4 I now pronounce you Internet and slave.
Type email here to subscribe to our newsletter.
© FOR ALL ETERNITY.

STICK
THAT
STAMP
HERE

30 Ways to Annoy Your Friends by Mail
Illustration © 2014 Ana Benaroya
from 120 Ways to Annoy Your Mother (and Influence People),
published by Thames & Hudson

Thames & Hudson

HOW TO BECOME A SHADOW OF THE PERSON YOU USED TO BE.
1 Run, run for your life. Get as far away from you as possible.
2 Write a breakup letter to yourself. It's over. Nothing will ever be the same again.
3 Only drink carbonated beverages.
4 Start a new, significantly more dull career.

STICK THAT STAMP HERE

30 Ways to Annoy Your Friends by Mail
Illustration © 2014 Ana Benaroya
from 120 Ways to Annoy Your Mother (and Influence People),
Published by Thames & Hudson

Thames & Hudson

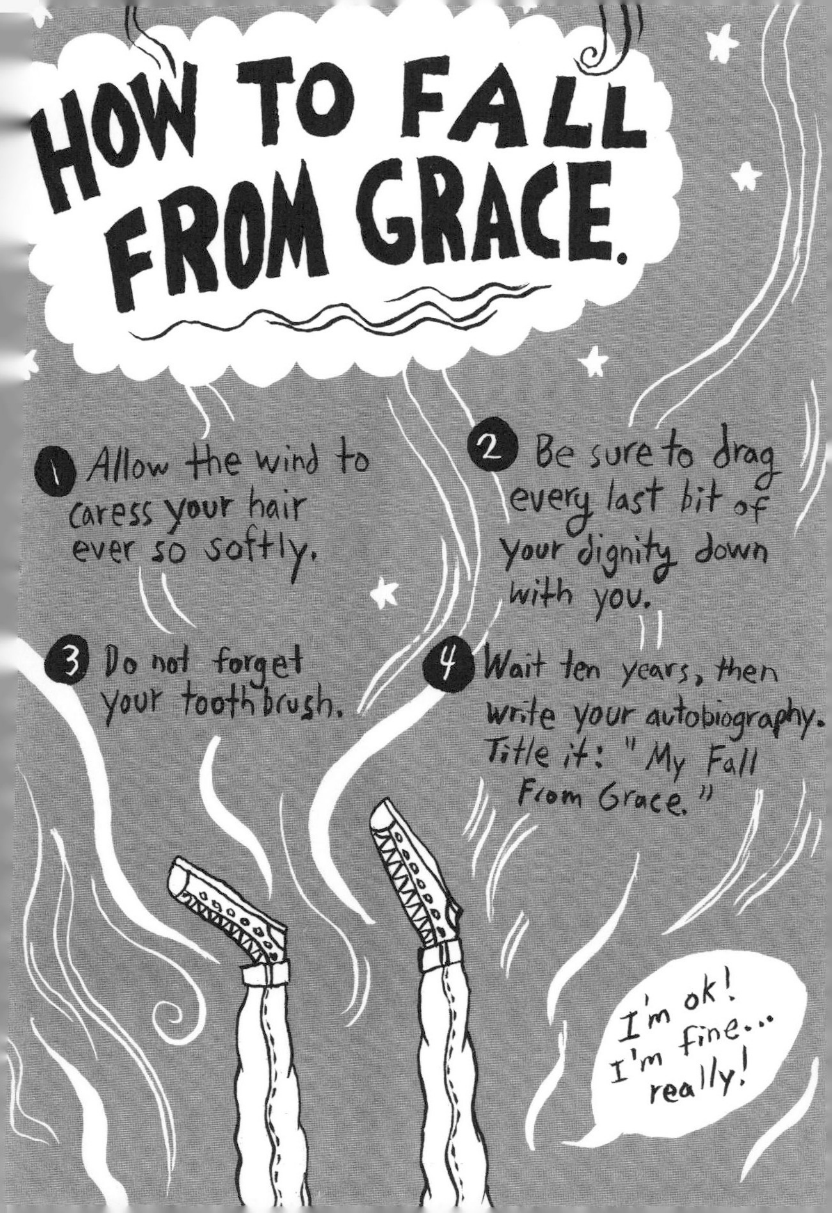
HOW TO FALL FROM GRACE.
1 Allow the wind to caress your hair ever so softly.
2 Be sure to drag every last bit of your dignity down with you.
3 Do not forget your toothbrush.
4 Wait ten years, then write your autobiography. Title it: "My Fall From Grace."
I'm ok! I'm fine... really!

STICK
THAT
STAMP
HERE

30 Ways to Annoy Your Friends by Mail
Illustration © 2014 Ana Benaroya
from 120 Ways to Annoy Your Mother (and Influence People),
published by Thames & Hudson

Thames & Hudson

1. Buy a really awesome spy hat.
2. Invent your own code language for communicating with the mother country.
3. Take mental notes with your eyes. It's all about being observant yet casual.
4. If ever questioned, tell people you had a nomadic youth and don't remember much of it.

STICK THAT STAMP HERE

30 Ways to Annoy Your Friends by Mail
Illustration © 2014 Ana Benaroya
from *120 Ways to Annoy Your Mother (and Influence People)*,
published by Thames & Hudson
Thames & Hudson

HOW TO BECOME SELF-SUFFICIENT.
1 To start, you need to grind your own coffee beans. None of that coffee bean grinder nonsense.
2 Put on your socks BEFORE you put on your underwear. Trust us on this one.
3 You will need to hunt for your own food. Consider moving into the local supermarket.
4 Somehow find a way to make decisions on your own.
I Know, I Know, it's excruciating.

STICK THAT STAMP HERE

30 Ways to Annoy Your Friends by Mail

from 120 Ways to Annoy Your Mother (and Influence People),
published by Thames & Hudson

Thames & Hudson

HOW TO BE REALLY AWKWARD. ← awkward period

1. Start every sentence with nervous laughter.

2. Stand either too close for comfort or too far away to be heard.

3. Do that thing where you play with your toenails while maintaining really intense eye contact.

4. Overshare during inopportune moments. (Ex: In an elevator, during long car journeys, etc.)

Well, isn't this empty space on the page a little awkward?

STICK THAT STAMP HERE

30 Ways to Annoy Your Friends by Mail
Illustration © 2014 Ana Benaroya
From 120 Ways to Annoy Your Mother (and Influence People),
published by Thames & Hudson
Thames & Hudson

HOW TO BE INTERESTING.
POOF!
1 Only speak every other day.
2 Stay unpredictable. Consistency eventually leads to assimilation.
3 Use horses as your only mode of transportation.
4 Always announce your weather prediction for the upcoming week. Continue to do so even if you are consistently wrong.

STICK
THAT
STAMP
HERE

30 Ways to Annoy Your Friends by Mail
Illustration © 2014 Ana Benaroya
from 120 Ways to Annoy Your Mother (and Influence People),
published by Thames & Hudson

Thames & Hudson

HOW TO PRETEND YOU ARE A FOREIGNER.

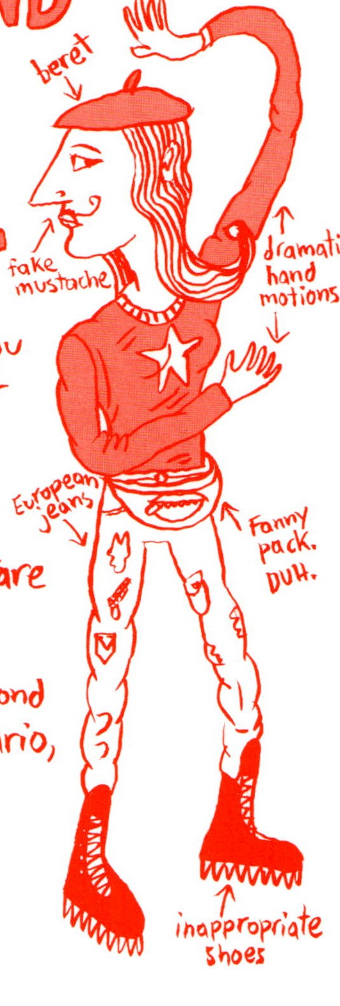

1. Be sure to keep your children out late. If you are a child, stay out past your bedtime.
2. Walk slower than the average pace of your city/town. Stop and stare frequently.
3. If possible, learn a second language. Worse case scenario, speak broken English.
4. Wear weather-inappropriate clothing.

STICK
THAT
STAMP
HERE

30 Ways to Annoy Your Friends by Mail
Illustration © 2014 Ana Benaroya
from 120 Ways to Annoy Your Mother (and Influence People),
published by Thames & Hudson

Thames & Hudson

HOW TO BE MYSTERIOUS.
WHAT?
WHO IS THAT?
OH, SHE'S MYSTERIOUS.
AN ENIGMA!
1 Speak infrequently and dress eccentrically.
2 Try and stay in the corners of rooms. Preferably in shadowy corners.
3 Appear lost in your thoughts at all times.
4 Live in an undesirable neighborhood on the outskirts of town.

STICK
THAT
STAMP
HERE

30 Ways to Annoy Your Friends by Mail

from 120 Ways to Annoy Your Mother (and Influence People),
published by Thames & Hudson

Thames & Hudson

HOW TO BE AN ARTIST.

1. Find a focus and REALLY, really focus on it. (Ex: Blue paintings of rare earthworm species.)

2. You must simultaneously be eccentric yet able to socialize with wealthy people.

3. Be sure to live in the artsy part of town. There is no such thing as an artist from the suburbs.

4. Choose friends who will add to your collectibility appeal. You need people at your openings who will make you and your paintings look better.

STICK THAT STAMP HERE

30 Ways to Annoy Your Friends by Mail

from 120 Ways to Annoy Your Mother (and Influence People),
published by Thames & Hudson

Thames & Hudson